The Art of Prospecting and Lead Generation

By: Jesse Rogers

I0473817

Bardic Productions – Copyright May 31, 2012

Table of Contents:

- Help Wanted
- Press Releases
  - Business wire
  - PR news Wire
- Relocation Announcements
- New Executive Announcements
- Venture Capital Announcements / Websites
- Building Directories / Business Parks
- Customer Websites
- Government Contract Awards
- Trade Shows
- Competitors
- Incoming Email
- Wikipedia
- Driving
- SIC Codes
- NAICS Codes
- Cage Codes

- Now you need a Name
  - Jigsaw
  - LinkedIN
  - Manta
  - Facebook
- Gatekeeper
- Your Companies Website

A word from the author:

The frontline of any company is going to be their sales team, without sales the company is going to flounder and die, if you go back through the history of any large company there is a small company and before the small company existed there was a person with an idea and he had to sell it to someone else. With that said and no matter where you are or which company you are with the art of developing new customers is the one constant throughout. It doesn't matter if you are selling a product or yourself, you are going to need to find people /companies to sell it to. The successful salesperson does not stand around waiting for opportunities to knock at their door, they go out into the hallways of life and find out where opportunity is and get to it before it enters someone else's door.

The idea behind this book is to put into simple words and actions the things you need to do to find opportunities and to develop new and lasting relationships with new potential customers. Using simple common sense methods and plain speak we will show you where you need to be looking and what you need to be doing with the information you find there.

We are not selling you any services, or any additional information, we are not prospecting you, we are simply delivering the goods, information and methodology to a pathway of successful lead generation.

Prospecting

The Art of Finding New Customers

When you think of the old miner who is digging in the dirt or panning for gold you are probably not very far off from the current day's business climate when it comes to finding potential customers. Whether your company provides a product or a service the art of finding customers is something that is essential to the wealth of your organization. As the saying goes "if you build a better mouse trap people will beat a path to your door" may be true to this day, but someone is going to have to show them where your door is located, how to open your door, and how the mouse trap is supposed to work.

The word prospecting is not directly defined by Webster's dictionary but leads to the word "explore," and thus the following definition makes sense: prospecting (v), to make or conduct a systematic search; prospect (n), a potential customer, client, or purchaser.

One of the key goals you must remember is that you want to make your customer or potential customer feel like they have your complete attention and that they are the only thing on your plate. They are going to think that there is nothing on your plate other then what they need, and we all know that is not the case but you have to make it seem it is.

Now you could take the easy way out and purchase your leads and good for you if you choose that way, it can be quite expensive, and these leads have probably been purchased before and have already been called by everyone and his brother, and besides what is the possibility they have the right people on the lists for you to be successful in your endeavors. Either way there is a better way to go about it, in fact for your specific industry you are going to have to do most of this anyway, so you might as well do it right from the start and save yourself some cash.

Leads

There are many definitions of what is considered a lead, from the simplest which would be a company name, to the most sophisticated which would be something that has been qualified and is ready to make a purchase this would include company name, contact name, phone number, job title, email address, the fact that they are in need of your product or service, and so on. Your journey on the path to finding leads will land you somewhere between the two above situations, more than likely you will lean more towards the first one than the second one, but that is just the start, finding a lead is just the beginning after you have found it you will have to nurture it very much like you would a plant and hope that it grows, but we will get into that a little later.

Where do you look?

Depending upon your position within your company you will be exposed to different situations and will have different types of tools that will be available to you for the efforts of locating and finding new customers. Since I don't know if you are an "Outside Salesperson" or and "Inside Sales Person" or "A Customer Service Representative" or "A Lead Farmer" or any other number of positions that would partake of the requirements of finding new customers I will try and include a little something for everyone. Realistically the process of finding new customers is something that pretty much can be done by anyone and should be done every waking moment of any given day. Now some people would find that very disturbing, talking about how important it is to separate work from home life and we all need some time to decompress and recharge our batteries. What I have to say to that is if you purchased this book you are not that person, you are someone who is interested in exploring every avenue of opportunity to be successful and my intent is to give you as many possible ways of finding potential customers as I can and if some of them seem strange or unusual then so be it, because it all comes down to finding that small piece of the puzzle that helps you find and make contact with a potential customer giving you the opportunity to close that sale, then the process starts all over again, or in reality continues as it always does.

Now prospecting can be done in any number of ways, the phone seems to work the best since you have the ability to contact many more people in the same time it would take to visit each potential new customer in person, why should you waste the time and money it takes for a visit if there is no viable reason for seeing a customer in person. There are times when it is necessary to visit with customers for no apparent reason other than to meet face to face and that is perfectly fine if you are selling large dollar products then usually the old school method of a handshake and looking someone in the eye can be very important to a potential customer and you should accommodate the customer accordingly.

In today's economy the best way to make a profit is often by saving a nickel or a dime. I once heard the story of JC Penny, the actual man not the store, he was in one of his stores and this was back when they would wrap your purchase up and tie it off with twine. He explained to the Sales Clerk that Profit was made by saving money on the twine that was used that was used to tie up the product. This statement holds true today in a world of ever shrinking profit margins, if you can save money on the overhead charges your ability to maintain a profit margin is greatly increased by that fact.

Other ways of prospecting would be "Snail" Mail, Sending out flyers, obtaining information from your website on visitors to your site, you could even tie a piece of paper to a rock and throw it threw a potential customers window. I wouldn't recommend that last one but you get the point that ways of prospecting are unlimited to your creative mind.

Currently one of the most easy ways to prospect is through the internet, there is so much information on line now a days that you could almost find everything you need right there. Of course there are some pitfalls to using the internet, such as there is no real way to know if the information you are finding is current or accurate. Often time's people give up using the information on the internet because of the amount of times that it turns out to be useless information but you can't look at it that way, you must see it as it is, information that you didn't have before. Many times just having a small amount of information is what you need to get your foot in the door so to speak.

Now the simple fact that you were able to find some useful information is only half the battle, you have to take that information and utilize it in a way that will lead to moving you a long a successful path in turning that prospect into a qualified potential customer, or in other words someone that is worth pursuing further. If you are a lead farmer or an inside sales person you would probably at this time after finding a qualified lead or a warm lead as they are sometimes referred to pass this along to an outside sales person who would then take over from there. The standard introduction would follow and then securing an appointment to do a face to face meeting with the potential client.

We all dream of a never ending supply of clients, that is what we are in business for after all clients means money and that is what we are trying to earn.

But before we get ahead of ourselves let us get back on track and start from the beginning and go over the whole process from start to finish.

The standard selling process goes something like this:

- Build Rapport
- Qualification
- Company Story
- Features / Benefits
- Closing

Cold Calling

Many people have multiple definitions of what cold calling actually is. I would define the act of cold calling as, whenever you are speaking with a potential client that is unknown to you. So with that you can include that to face to face, on the phone, or even when you send an unsolicited email to a potential client. The art of cold calling is to be able to demonstrate your ability to present yourself in a socially acceptable manner to an unknown client. It is very much like when you are new to an area and you are trying to meet new people and to make new friends. When it comes down to the business world it isn't very much different because you are pretty much trying to do the same things only in the business world we call that building rapport or building relationships. It is much easier to secure business from someone who likes you then from someone who doesn't like you; you will often hear these people called pushers and blockers. A pusher is someone you can count on to put in a good word for you or to push your product or service forward in his company, a blocker would be someone of the opposite persuasion they will put up obstacles for your product or service denying you access to the right people or will blatantly speak against you, your company, or your product or service. Just keep in mind that a friend is worth more than an enemy and as such you do not want to do or say something that would make a potential friend feel that they do not want to be your friend.

Now there are a number of people out there stating that "Cold Calling" is dead that a good sales person shouldn't be doing cold calling, in fact there are a few that have mentioned they would fire there sales person if they were caught cold calling. That in a nutshell is just plain stupid, too often is the case that sales people do not want to do cold calling, mostly because they find the task difficult or even beneath them. Our society has become so complacent in the fact that they want the easy path one hundred percent of the time and they wonder why they cannot be successful when it is plain as day they have to learn to do what it takes to be successful. We have gotten so used to being spoon fed from the cherry tree of clients that when the cherries are all gone we would rather wait right there under the tree for the cherries to come back rather than go look for a different cherry tree, or some different fruit all together. If you want to be successful you have to learn to think out of the box and part of that is hunting down and finding new potential revenue streams where your product or service would be found useful by a client. This is all really just plain common sense, which is obviously far afield from what so many sales people feel is part of their job description these days. The key about being successful with Cold Calling comes down to time management, you should not be cold calling or prospecting one hundred percent of the time, mostly because this is a long sale process and will not yield the cherries you will need to fill your short term quota's. You will still have to call upon, visit, and service your traditional existing client base else you will lose that client base for lack of attention. With that said you will need to manage the amount of time you do spend prospecting and cold calling, the idea is to constantly be adding to the top of your sales funnel so that your sales funnel is constantly filled with existing and new potential clients. Else you will find yourself in the position of having an empty sales funnel which usually leads to a career change on your part by the request of your Sales Manager.

When to Prospect?

Did you ever consider how ridiculous it would be to try to cram on a farm - to forget to plant in the spring, relax all summer, and then cram in the fall to bring in the harvest? The farm is a natural system. The price must be paid and the process followed. You always reap what you sow; there is no shortcut.

The simple truth is not many people like to prospect; it takes up time that could otherwise be used doing a number of other things that could be more profitable for the individual or company. Of course that sentiment is all fine and dandy if you have a never ending list of customers beating your door down to purchase your product or service, and we all know there are not too many of those companies out there these days.

So with that in mind the best thing to do is to set aside a little time each day to do some prospecting, it is best to move that time around don't always do it at ten o'clock, fluctuate the time frames you will have a better chance of catching a person at their desk if you do it that way. You have to remember the people you are calling upon have their own jobs to take care of and even if your product or service will make their jobs easier or more efficient, their time is valuable to them, so keep that in mind when you are prospecting. If you can track when you try and make contact with a potential prospect this way you can adjust your calling times to try and catch them at the most appropriate time of day.

The other thing to realize is that the initial phone call is not designed to make a sale, that first contact is far away from a closing opportunity for you, I mean it can happen but you should expect it to right from the get go. The first contact is an introduction of who you are and what you have to offer this potential customer. Many times you may simply get hung up on, or told we are not interested or some other negative type statement. This is something that you should not deter you from the act of prospecting, many people let that negativity affect them and that is not a good thing for any type of person in sales.

There are many people who think that the art of Prospecting is a dying art, and that is fine but it is still an art, and if you can learn it you will be better off down the road. Besides if there are fewer people out there prospecting leaves more room for those of us who are out there doing it.

One of the things you should be doing is staying up to date on what your customers are staying up to date on. You should be reading the same things they are, subscribing to the same newsletters they would. Stay up to date on the same current events that affect them and their businesses so you can demonstrate your knowledge and be able to talk with good sense when you communicate with them about your products and services that will aid with their products and services. Besides by keeping up to date on the business of the day, you can use that to help in the continued development of your relationship with the potential customer.

Try creating a reading list pick five things that would be a value to have in your pocket, you will be surprised how you can use the things you learn in books, magazines, even some business television shows, to help in finding solutions or opportunities to better your relationship with a new potential client. It also helps in that you can speak on the subject matters that may come up in a simple conversation you would have with a prospect, this way if he/she mentions something about their industry it would be helpful if you knew what they were talking about and could answer like someone with knowledge on your side, that will get you a little further down the road of relationship building.

Remember what the goal is for the call, are you trying to set up a meeting, send some information to them, tell them about your website, or are you trying to get the name of the appropriate person to speak with about your products, the decision maker.

Where to start?

To start with do not call you best prospects first, the reason is simple if you are just starting at prospecting you don't want to make a simple mistake or come across as not being professional or knowledgeable about what you are speaking of. If you were to do that with your best prospects right off the bat you could lose some good potential customers that way. You are always going to run into glitches as you practice and refine your pitch so start off with you "B" or even "C" accounts till you feel comfortable with your pitch.

One of the things you are going to run into right away, probably even on that first phone call is "Voicemail", like I said earlier people are working and doing their jobs and many times that means they are not sitting at their desk waiting to receive your phone call. So you should be prepared for the inevitable and know what you are going to do if you get their voicemail. I would hesitate from leaving a voice mail on that first call, if you are following the guidelines from earlier you will try back a few times at different times to see if you can catch them at their desk. In the event that you can't get them say after the third try I would go ahead and leave a voicemail at that time.

You should know what you want to say even on a voicemail and have a separate script ready for that specific purpose, and if you are not good at talking off the cuff then you should have that script written down so you can read it.   Make sure you practice any scripts that you read so you can read them easily without flubbing over anything, sometimes you only get one shot at a voicemail, at the same time you should not leave very long voicemails because plain and simply people won't listen to it once they realize you are trying to sell something to them.

With that same pretense in mind you should also have a good idea of what you are going to say just on the chance that someone actually answers the phone, after all that is you goal in the first place. You don't want to be surprised when someone on the other end says "Hello". Same principles apply to a live person as they do with the voicemail, be prepared, have a script, write it down if you have to, they are not going to know that it is the same thing you say to everyone on the phone when you call them, but at the same time don't make it obvious that you are reading something to them practice the script before getting on the phone so you are comfortable with it. The idea is to work yourself away from the script so that you will sound more genuine and knowledgeable about what you are talking about.

One very important thing to remember is to not let yourself use the word, or more accurately the sound of "UM", when someone hears this word or sound it is very obvious that you are searching for the right thing to say next and makes you sound less knowledgeable then you want to come across as. The word or sound "UM" means "I don't know", and the key thing is to "Know" everything.

The other thing you will come up against is the standard. "We don't want any", or "We are happy with our current vendor". Each time you run up against something like this you "MUST" write it down and take the time to develop a rebuttal for it. Now keep in mind rebuttals don't always work but you need to be able to say something to try and keep the conversation going so that you can get over that immediate hurdle and take back control of the conversation.

Conversations are like a game, and if you don't have any answers to whatever they may hit you with you are going to lose the game and the conversation will end and so will your chances with that potential customer. You are not going to win every conversation so don't even worry about it, but you need to always be making your tools that will help you win a greater amount of the conversation games that you come up against.

You have to approach prospecting as a learning experience every phone call, every email, or face to face is going to teach you something, either about yourself or about the potential client, and you have to take that feedback and dust it off, paint over the ugly parts and recycle it to make you a better salesperson, if you don't you will continue to drive into the same pot holes that you always do and it will be that much harder for you to be successful in your position with your company.

Sometimes it is not what you are saying but how you are saying it, experiment try different things and always learn from your mistakes. Most important is don't get yourself worked up over mistakes, learn to laugh at yourself for the blunders you do, it's ok it will help with the negativity that we all face in sales. Don't be afraid to ask questions, this will let you potential customer become engaged in the conversation more fully and it will give you a chance to listen and learn about what is going on at this company, usually they will discuss the things they would like to see different or products that they are having problems with and you need to pay attention here because your next step would be to help find a solution for those problems and it will give you a chance to introduce a product or service that could be a first step to initiating a sale and turning that prospect into a customer.

Questions lead to a longer conversation and the longer the conversation the better chance you have of warming this cold lead up a bit. It will also give you the opportunity to help learn about who may be the decision maker in the company that would be the one who actually says "Yes" to making a purchase of your product or service. Many managers leave it up to the key people doing the work, others want to be involved in the process, and still others have nothing to do with the process and it is left up to the bean counters in the purchasing department.

Don't try to own the conversation that will usually lead to losing the opportunity that you are so desperately trying to put together. Initial phone calls should be brief, like I stated before you are not trying to sell something on the first phone call, there will be other calls, remember you are trying to build a relationship. Try not to sound nervous, that will be heard in the way that you speak. Usually the more talking the prospect does the better off you are. When you do get a chance to ask questions ask good ones that

don't get answered with a yes or a no,
but more like:
What are the challenges you face in your position?
How would you define success?
What problems have you faced in the past with products or services like ours?

Things that will get him/her to open up and discuss things with you.

Keep in mind there will be times that you will come across those people who will open up and discuss with you almost anything, they will love discussing all the problems that they have faced and be interested in how you could help to fix them and they will never by a thing from you. Once you identify these prospects you will have to handle them carefully in the future or find an alternate contact at the company to further make inroads.

Always keep in mind that this is a long sales cycle from prospect to customer. It is believed that you have to contact a potential customer many times before you can move them forward even the first step, most people give up early in the process and never get to the point of moving them forward because they have given up on the potential customer.

Prospecting is about achieving critical mass in your search don't let it fall by the wayside because you are not getting the immediate satisfaction that you desire. Keep with it, it will pay off in the end.

The most important thing is to catalog the information you obtain in your phone calls so when you come back to them at a later date you can pick up from where you left off rather than have to start from scratch and if the potential customer on the other side remembers your last phone call they may wonder how much you really care about them if you keep asking the same questions each time you call.

Existing Clients

Now that we have gone over how to call a little let us talk about who to call for a bit.

If you have an existing client base then you are lucky you already have some calling material right there in front of you. Like I mentioned earlier we have basically have three categories of existing clients, those would be:

"A" – this would be a customer who is currently buying from you in the current year.
"B" – this would be a customer that purchased something from you last year but hasn't this year.
"C" – this would be a customer that has purchased from you more than a year ago, and you haven't heard anything from them since.

The main reason I always recommend you starting with your existing client base is simple you have already established a relationship with them if not you specifically your company has and that is good enough to make them warm. They already know your company and more importantly your products, and that will be the thing that gets your foot in the door.

So start with your "B" and "C" accounts, take the time to learn the history with them, if you can find out why they stopped purchasing your product or service you will be well served with that information. Some companies may have faced a slowdown, other companies may have transitioned on to something else and your product or service is no longer applicable, and then there is always the possibility that they had a very bad experience with your company and specifically chose to use a competitor because of that experience. It is always fun to step into that situation without knowing the history, they are usually more than happy to bring you up to speed on that bad taste they obviously still have in their mouths. Again don't panic if something like that happens use your most important tool at your disposal and that is to "Listen", more than likely someone along the line chose not to listen and that is probably why you are in this position now. Also don't make promises, customers with a bad taste in their mouth do not want to hear promises they want to see action and resolution, but I get ahead of myself.

The main thing you want to do with regard to "B" and "C" customers is to re-engage them find out what they have been up to, discover the changes to their organizations, maybe they had personnel changes and the new guy/girl didn't even know about your company.

Now granted this is more about Customer Care Strategies, but it is still one of the most important things you could do, the whole idea about getting a new customer is to retain that customer, which is why we start at with these "B" and "C" accounts so we can gather a better understanding about how to do just that down the line.

Think of it as simply checking in with your customer to see how they are, and if you are new to this customer giving them an introduction to you. Providing them with your contact information if you are new is a great way to begin cultivating that new relationship with this previous customer. If you are aware of what they had purchased in the past you should bring that up to see how things are working with the products they have of yours. By following up on purchases it shows you being pro-active, rather than re-active, customers truly appreciate that more then you could ever know. It shows genuine concern, of course if they have a problem with your product or service don't even think about asking them to purchase something else until you have resolved the problem they have, that is not only poor salesmanship but it is also very insulting and a customer will remember that for a long time.

Now since these are "B" and "C" accounts you need to investigate gently why they haven't been back to purchase more of your products or services. Any feedback that they give you at this point should be documented so you can use it to alter your approach on how you proceed further, and it could be useful information to your immediate supervisor or even the management team to make sure things are addressed that could make your product or service better for customers down the road.

The key is to learn as much about the account and the environment as possible so that you can access what products in your arsenal would be good to present to them and to the appropriate people in their organization. Depending upon what your company is selling, you may have multiple contacts at the same company that do different things, and if you don't you should always be trying to make new contacts at the company the worst position you could be in is to only have a single contact for an organization and then that person retires or leaves and you are faced with starting over from scratch with them.

As many companies have seen in these tough economic times a slow down or decline in orders from your customers or even worse if you are in danger of losing a customer, you can utilize the phone calls with them to assess the situation and see if appropriate measures can be taken to resolve problems and demonstrate your dedication to the customer and retain them rather then having to go out and find a new customer to replace the one you lost.

Once you have gone through your "B" and "C" accounts you should be following up on shipments to your "A" accounts so you can follow up with them, this again shows your active client that you are pro-active in wanting to learn about their experience with your company, and gives you an opportunity to correct mistakes before they fester and become dangerous to your relationship with this "A" company.

Something else you gain by following up with "A" companies is when they have something good to say about your product or service. When you get good feedback be sure to pass it along to your Production Group or Service Group, for not only do you have to cultivate an externally good relationship with your customers you also have to cultivate an internally good relationship with those that deliver the product or service to your customers. Do you really think they only want to hear about the bad stuff, they will truly appreciate good feedback from a customer and if you are the one delivering that good information they will look upon you more favorably and that will make it easier for you to get the assistance you need from them so you can service your customers.

New Leads

So now that you have gone through your existing clientele you should be much more comfortable speaking on the phone and in your production of emails that showcase your product or service in a good light. So what is next? Well now you have to actually get your hands dirty and start mining new leads that you can make contact with, this will not happen overnight so the first thing you need to do is figure out the best way to keep the information that will begin piling up organized. There are many programs out there that are available for purchase that are specifically designed for keeping contact lists organized. You can do some research online and find out what each one has to offer, it may be that your company has a specific program they prefer their employees to utilize for this effort. I personally am a big believer in Excel, it is a very powerful program that will allow you to organize things in the way that you find most useful, very simply put if you can't access the information you put into the program in an easy time efficient way then you are not using the right program for you. In a nutshell what you are trying to capture is at a minimum the following information

Company Name

Company Address

Company Website

Company Phone Number

Contact Name

Contact Title

Contact Email Address

It is also good to have some field where you can put notes, keep track of when the last time you tried to make contact with them and how (phone or email), other things that could be helpful would be, a place for a second phone number like a cell phone, maybe a place to indicate what product or service they would be interested in, things like that go a long way when you come back to a contact you haven't called in a while. Aside from that you can add additional columns for other information you need based upon your own unique situation. If you have real Excel Skills there are a number of other things you can do to automate some really cool things for your list, but that is another subject matter altogether.

A good lead would be any company or person that may have an interest in the products and services that you have to offer. Sounds pretty simple but you will find as you dig further and further into lead generating that your net can get quite big in what it is trying to capture. Sure in the beginning you will be capturing obvious companies that deal with your products and services but as continue to gather information you will find that you will continue to broaden your search as you try and reach untapped market segments or even whole new industries.   You will do this by staying on top of regional and national business sources and look for opportunities that your company can fill for these potential clients. When you are selling you are always narrowing your list of potential clients down to a smaller group that is more likely to be interested in the product or service you are selling as you move them down your sales funnel.

In lead generation you are constantly widening your circle of nets in order to catch a larger group of people / companies that you can try and qualify. Simply put you are working the numbers and the more numbers you have to start with will give you a greater opportunity to sell more.

Referrals

One thing that is often overlooked when prospecting is the value that your clients have for you and the company that you represent. The value of a relationship that you cultivate over time comes in real handy for this aspect of finding new customers. If you have a good customer that is happy with you, and with your company, and with your product, you should face no objections from them if you were to ask them about other companies in the area that may be interested in your service or products. They can be one of your biggest lead generators right off the bat, they probably know more about the region and what companies are doing what, much more then you may and people in specific industries usually mingle with each other over the years as people move from company to company, I have some customers that I could write their resumes for them as I have dealt with them at many different companies over the years. They often do not have any issues with letting you know who else is using the product you are selling. You can even go one step further and ask for a recommendation or maybe an introduction that often carries a lot of weight with someone. One thing to remember is that this can also back fire on your and if you do a bad job with the next guy it could have ramifications on the relationship you have with the person who recommended you in the first place. So use this advice cautiously when working with people.

Undergoing Changes

As I mentioned earlier about reading and staying on top of current business news and business climates you will often come across information that will help you to identify potential clients.

You may find out about a change in upper management, about a new product, or maybe a purchase of or the sale of a company to another. Changes of this type often bring opportunity to get your foot in the door as new procedures and policies may be put in place that you can utilize to get that opportunity you couldn't before. Keep your eyes open for key things like this so that you can be prepared to take advantage of them when they pop up.

If you are dealing with manufacturing companies, you always hear about companies winning this contract or that contract, well that information is well worth looking into to see if this will affect the facilities in your area, which could lead to an opportunity and by getting in their first and being prepared you may not even have to face off against your competition who may have been sitting on the side lines oblivious to what was going on.

The Search

So where do you find these leads, I know I have been talking about a lot of things so far, but I am sure you are now very much interested in the actual location of these new leads.

Well now that you have a better understanding of a number of things that are important to the process of prospecting we can now tell you some of the in's and out's of finding the lead.

Start by looking at your current clients to find new ones.

When I say this I am referring to other business that is available at a location you are currently doing business with, such as a different department or division, there may be more business right in front of you but you never knew about it because you never looked for it. So take a look at your current customers and ask the people you have already developed relationships with and see what else is still on the table at their company, you may be surprised at what you find.

Networking

If you do any type of networking I would go there next, these again are people that you know or that know you and as such would be your best place to find out about new business opportunities. Many should be able to recommend you as well, but again be careful you don't want to ruin a relationship just to get another one.

Buying a list of leads

You could simply buy a list of leads there are plenty of companies out there that will gladly sell you a list of company contacts and they do try to get it right, but now you could be spending money for something that you could easily do yourself, prices can vary greatly, and you can never be sure how many times they may have already sold this information so I wouldn't suggest this as your best opportunity for lead generation.

Direct Mail

Of course to do this you would pretty much already have to have a list to be able to send a direct mail out and I don't know about you but most direct mail stuff just ends up in the trash business or personal. It is still a viable form of getting your companies information into the building but after that you really never know where it goes after that. The costs for this need to be measured carefully to ensure you are getting the bang for the buck and that the return is worth the effort.

Research

This is so important that I am going to say it again.

Research.

Researching companies and gathering information so you can contact them appropriately, is by far the best way to go about generating your own leads, it gives you the greatest amount of control and since you are not spending any extra money it is a much better bang for your buck. Before I get into some greater detail about the research aspect I want to talk to you about some other media forms that will give you some good insight when you are doing some of your research.

National Public Radio

If you are listening to music or talk radio, on your way to or from work you really need to stop it. NPR is a great resource for what is going on at a global scale with regard to world events and business, and it is just a very interesting show to listen to. You will learn a lot about a lot of things, many things before they even hit the main stream news media which could give you an up on your competitors knowing the same information which could mean the difference between winning a customer and not. You will not go wrong by listening to public radio, in fact you will be surprised how much you become ahead of the standard news curve that your friends, customers, and family are on.

Newspapers, Radio, Television

The traditional media outlets are still a better source then nothing for business and world news. I mean knowing what is going on in the business world is key to hearing about new contracts, sales and purchases, new products and so on. Obviously depending upon your industry world events could play a very major role in how you market your business, and to whom.

Trade Magazines

If you are in a specific industry that has trade publications then you should be either getting them delivered or at least reading them online so you can stay abreast of things specifically dealing in your industry.

Online E-Zines and Industry Newsletters

Again these things would be very specific to your industry and as such are a good source of material to find new leads in. This is usually the cutting edge for the industry on changes, updates, business sales and mergers.

Industry White Papers

They always list the author and the company they work for so if you can find one on something that deals with your industry, product, or service then you now have a specific lead you may be able to utilize to find the appropriate person at the company.

New Product Introduction

If there is a new product out there that is being introduced it has to be manufactured or designed somewhere, there are a lot of things that go into a new product that have nothing to do with the product itself such as marketing and legal documents, so NPI's as they are referred to are a good thing to know about regardless of your product or service.

Company Purchases and Mergers

When a company goes through a purchase or merger there are usually changes that occur people are let go others are brought on, facilities are moved, new ones are opened, others are closed, all this is again good information for finding opportunities.
Ok those were some ideas for finding some easy information that is readily available to you.

Now let us get back to researching.

Google / Bing / Yahoo

It doesn't really matter which search engine you like to utilize they all pretty much operate off of Boolean Parameters, so include pertinent information in your search field.

For example: Let's say you are selling something to do with Printed Circuit Boards and you cover the state of Alabama.

In your search field you would type in "printed circuit boards Alabama"

This will give you a return of printed circuit board companies in Alabama, it will include a lot more things like companies that do business in Alabama as well so depending upon your sales territory you may need to weed through some of your listing to make sure you are getting useful information.

You can change the keywords around trying different things to narrow your searching always include the state so you want else you will get quite a lot of information you may not want.

The Results can be overwhelming and it can fraught with duplication but you are looking at a lot of raw data that needs to be sorted and cataloged and put into useful formats.

If the results are too many to handle you can always save the search and come back to it as time allows. The main goal at this point is to document the companies that you find and start building your list don't try and do it all at one time, this is a process, not a candy store.

Websites for companies

One of the things you will find in your search results are websites that offer a sorted list of companies in specific industries this can be very helpful to you since someone has done most of the sorting for you. I continue to find new ones each time I am doing website research, but these are just a few that I find to be helpful in my own work. You should always check out new ones that you come across just to see what they are offering, don't be afraid to give up the one you are currently using for a better one.
Some of these websites are:

www.thomasnet.com

www.manta.com

www.macraesbluebook.com

www.company.com

www.yellowpages.com

www.iqsdirectory.com

www.mfg.com

www.hotfrog.com

www.businessprofiles.com

www.kellysearch.com

www.citysearch.com

www.superpages.com

www.nearstop.com

www.d2pbuyersguide.com

www.thebusinessportal.com

Plus man more..

Once in one of these websites you will find ways to expand or narrow your search parameters to meet your requirements for the specific industry that you are trying to research. These websites will provide you with some very good information, specifically they will usually give you Company address, phone, fax, website. Many will even include what they do, industries they serve, yearly sales, number of employees and more. It is rare but some of the websites are now even providing contacts as well, but we will get to that a little later.

Help Wanted

If you are working with a specific job title, say like a "Test Engineer" or "Administrative Assistant" you could check some of the job sites, like Monster or Career Builder and search for the job title and see who is looking to hire someone that meets that job title, if they are looking for someone that you are also looking for then there is a good chance that you want to be engaging this company as a sales lead since they may have a need for what you are selling. This is one of those ones that are often overlooked because many people who prospect never think outside of the box.

Press Releases

Major press releases for the business community can be found at:

www.businesswire.com

www.prnewswire.com

This is a great single stop place to find out what is going on right that moment in the business community. Don't be afraid to look, you never know what you will find and when you will find it.

Relocating Announcements

We touched on this a little earlier, but many companies are moving to new locations and as such if one was to come into your area it would be good to know about it so you can be prepared to engage with this company. This could be helpful to you in another way as well, if you see a company is relocating to a new location and it is not in your sales area, then make mention of it to the person who covers that area, and make sure you copy your boss as well, so he/she can see you are a team player, and the salesperson who you give this lead to kind of now owes you one in return.

New Executive Announcements

Someone new at the company, say a new Vice President of Engineering, well if this fits into the people you are working with at other companies then it would be good to engage this company as well since new people often like to institute changes when they take over.

Venture Capital Announcements – Venture Capital Websites

How do you know if a company is in a growth mode? Well if they are getting big investments that could very well be a sign to look a little deeper. Venture Capital Announcements may very well contain useful information and insight into the company you are looking at, this could include location information, or possibly even a name that you could utilize. The same is true with a Venture Capital Website, many sites are proud to display a list of customers they do business with as a sign of accomplishment. That list will provide you with the potential of learning of a company you may not have heard of before and as such are worth investigating.

Building Directories / Business Parks

If you travel in your sales position to visit with clients it is always a great idea to look at the building directory that they may operate out of, often like companies do business in the same area and as such you could identify a potential customer right down the hallway. The same is true with the business parks, though it may be more like a potential customer is in another building. Right the names down you see on the signs and when you get sometime look up what they do to further qualify a potential client.

Customer Websites

For the customers that you currently have and the potential customers that you know of, always take a moment to go thru their websites at least once or twice a year depending upon how regularly they update them. Your goal is to make sure that you see what customers that they are doing business with, because your product or service may appeal to their needs as well. All you have to do is add the company to your list this way you don't forget about it and it will eventually be investigated as you go down your list.

Government Contract Awards

The Government spends a lot of money so when an contract winner is announced it is worth listening to so you can see if the winning company could use your product or service. Sometimes contracts can take a lot of time in Engineering or Design and as such this lead isn't ready yet. When the right time comes around you will at least have it in your database rather than forgotten because you didn't write it down six months ago when you first heard about it.

Trade Shows

These events are a great way to add to a list of potential customers and they often come pre-qualified. If your company is running a booth you have a sign in log and as such potential customers who have an interest in your product are going to sign that log and give you there contact information. On the other hand if you are visiting a convention every booth operator is a potential customer to you and as such you gather information and see which ones are the best to approach about your own product or service. This would also include the people in attendance at the event as well, you can learn a lot by just listening, of course there is a time for that but there also comes a time where you will need to use some of your skill set and actually start up a conversation with some of them. It is a great time for face to face meetings to find new customers. Lastly there are those times when you cannot attend a trade show for whatever reason, you can however get a list of the companies in attendance at the event simply from a short visit to the events website, they pretty much always list the companies on the site.

Competitors

Utilizing a method we went over a little earlier, it is more than likely that your competitors have a list of customers on their own website, now that information would be considered pre-qualified since you probably can sell your product or service to your competitor's customers. I would put any information gleaned here a little higher on the priority list for investigation and further qualification. The same could be said for your customer's competitors, if they make or do the same thing as they do, then there is an overly good chance that you should be communicating with them.

Incoming Email

Whenever you receive legitimate email you should make it a point to be collecting those email addresses and the companies that the person who sent you the email works for. If you are already communicating with someone via email then you have an established relationship no matter how weak. You will be surprised how much information is delivered right to our doorstep, make sure you capture it.

This is one of those ones that so many people miss out on, if you are communicating with someone often times the CC: other people from there company on the email, you need to add those people to your list and contact them at a later date or for other reasons down the road.

Wikipedia

This is a great source of information dealing with quite a large amount of companies and industries, often you can find complete historical information on both companies and industries. This can be very helpful when trying to understand the history of the people you are trying to sell to, as well as possibly identifying new players that you were previously unaware of.

Driving

If you travel by car during your sales duties, you drive past quite a number of companies every time you are in the car, for those companies that you don't recognize with the full parking lots could be somebody who could use your product or service. Now I am not recommending that you do something reckless and write and drive at the same time, but however you can get that information documented in your database is what counts. As I mentioned previously you don't have to look it up right away but the simple fact that it is on your list gives it the best shot of being investigated and qualified. Always look for the full parking lots, that means they are doing something right.

SIC Codes – Standard Industrial Classification –

www.siccode.com

If you can identify a specific SIC code that identifies what would be your customer then this information could be very helpful as you can search specific to that code and your potential customer can be easily found in this manner. Often there are number of codes that could help identify potential leads for you.

NAICS Codes – North American Industry Classification System – www.naics.com

This is very similar to the SIC code and the same information can be gleaned from the site if you can identify your potential customer base by one of the NAICS codes.

Cage Codes

Anyone who sells anything to the United States Military must have a unique code that will identify the company from anyone else. There are many websites that list these companies by code, the listings can be quite extensive and you may have to sort the information for your particular area or industry. Either way there is a wealth of information here.

http://www.newportaero.com/home/manuals/cage/browse

If you have done some of the things spoken of earlier you will find your list of potential customers growing rather rapidly, quite possibly to a scary level, stop and take a breath, you will work through the list of potential customers as time permits. Just remember to update and fill in the blanks when you find out new and useful information that will help you move from a cold contact to an established relationship and business customer.

Something else that is important, don't delete companies that don't pan out or that turn out to be closed. This is still valuable information since the last thing you want to do is to discover this same company a year or so later and go through the process of finding this same information out once again. That would be a total waste of your time, better to indicate in the database that the company is closed or not a potential customer and for what reason.

Now you need a Name:

Ok so now what you should have in front of you is a list of your existing customers, you should also have a list of companies with some contact information such as a website or and address or a phone number. More than one thing that you don't have is a contact name, often you can call the company and ask for a specific department or manager, sometimes the receptionist can be quite helpful, often times you are confronted with a computer telephone system and you won't even get the opportunity to speak to a person. What would be great right about now would be a name, any name would probably get you somewhere. Well that is what we are going to discuss now.

Websites like Jigsaw, Manta, LinkedIN, and Lead411 can be very helpful in giving you what you need.

www.jigsaw.com

www.manta.com

www.linkedin.com

www.lead411.com

There are other sites out there as well but I have found these to be the most rewarding in my own contact information searching. The one I utilize the most is Jigsaw, it offers you the greatest return on the time you are putting in. I suggest that you join all of these sites if you have not already done so. You just type in the name of the company and presto if they have it in their database you can see a lot about the company including different locations throughout the world; often there are phone numbers for the other locations as well. The best part is you can search for different job titles or utilize the standard ones they have on the site and simply click on them and it will display contact names, job titles and state location of where they are located. Guess what? Now you have a name you can ask for when the receptionist asks who you would like to speak to. You can take it a step further and buy the contact right then and there, they have different levels of membership where you can buy the contact with cash or you can buy it with points you earn by inputting information that you may have that the website does not have. Either way they will give you the email address and phone number for the person if you buy it. This can be very helpful if you have multiple contacts at the same company in being able to fill in quite a lot of blanks. Now of course this information may be old as companies are dynamic and things are changing all the time and things do not get updated as much you would think. So do get upset if you call and that person doesn't work there anymore or isn't in that department anymore. You are dealing with investigating and qualifying, it doesn't take to many good leads to outweigh the bad leads.

If the company doesn't come up in jigsaw by putting the name in the search bar, then if you know the website you can click on Find Companies and you can then put the website in and find it that way, sometimes that comes in handy because the name they go by can be either different then what was entered into the system, or it may have been bought out by another company and is no longer listed under the name you know it by.

Of course there are going to be companies that don't come up in Jigsaw, and as such you should move on to a different site like Manta, they are now starting to list contacts when you look up the company, it is not a very extensive list but they do have quite a bit more companies in there system then Jigsaw so you may still get something you can use.

Now if you are still not finding anything you can move on to LinkedIN, you can do a company search in this website and if you have a reasonable amount of friends in LinkedIN you should be able to find some information you didn't have before. You can also join LinkedIN on their pay service and you would be able to introduce yourself to potential customers. The thing about LinkedIN that is so important is that each time you get a new friend on the site, you can view your new friends list of friends and by doing that you can then find other people to become friends with as well as find new companies and contacts at those companies that should go in your database. Are you starting to see how everything is sort of connected with each other? LinkedIN is like Facebook for the business world, take some time and look around join some discussion groups that have to do with your product or service or better yet start some new ones and see who you can attract that could be a potential customer for you.

So let's talk a little bit about LinkedIN, this is another great website that allows you to make new contacts and operates very much like Facebook does, you can search for people you know, and make a connection with them, you can also import your Gmail, or Outlook address book and they can find your existing connections that way. When you have exhausted making connections that way you have to do it the old fashioned way and that is looking at your connections, connections and seeing if any of them are good candidates for your product or service, this could be accomplished by looking at what company they work for or by what position they have listed as their job title. If you operate within a specific territory they will also list a general area from where the connection is based out of. Now you can request a connection often times without much of a hassle but the connection still has to approve your request, but once they have you now have the ability to look at their connections and see if you can add to your connections through your new connection. I know it sounds like a lot of connections going on and it is but it is worth the time and effort to do this as you now have a full name their job title, company name, and so forth, great information to add to you ever growing list of potential customers. Once a connection is made you will receive an email stating that you are now connected with this new person, I don't always have time to go and look at every new connections, connections so I usually make a folder in my outlook so that I can come back later and be able to click on view profile and go through these new connections. Often times when people sign up for LinkedIN they use their work email address which is great for you since now you know the email format for the company you are looking at, so moving forward you can probably deduce other potential customers email addresses for this company.

Now if you are trying to find a specific person doing a particular job, you can click on the company name and it will show you all of the employees of that company that are on LinkedIN, you don't always get the full names, much of that is dependent on how removed these other people are from your own connections. So the lesson you want to take away from this is that the more connections you have the better you are.

Another way of finding potential customers through LinkedIN is through the discussion groups they have on the site. This is also a good place to discuss your own products or services if they are applicable to the discussion that is going on, often times you may be able to solve a potential customers problem which will give you much credibility and make a cold contact much warmer when you approach him in person or call him on the phone.

Remember it is all about creating an nurturing relationships, most people will prefer to do business with someone they like or have an established relationship, worst case you will at least know you are in a position to get a shot at upcoming opportunities. The other thing to remember is that connections established through LinkedIN are yours, not your companies, so if you change jobs you still have those connections that will come with you. If you have a good relationship with a customer or a customer gives you some praise for the work that you did for them then don't be afraid to ask them to write a recommendation for you on LinkedIN, this will increase your credibility on the website and may help you if you are looking for another job, it is pretty much a win win on LinkedIN so make sure you utilize this site for your own benefit.

Manta

The one thing that Manta is good for more than anything else is in finding addresses and phone numbers if I can't find something on Jigsaw and the Google is just giving me the main website which does not have contact information for the local facility in my area, then I will go to Manta which has probably the most comprehensive list of companies. Depending upon what you are looking for this can be a lot to go through if they have a lot of sales offices or design offices, but when you have nowhere else to go Manta is a great resource.

They have been getting better about having contact information but it doesn't compare to Jigsaw in that regard but you never know and when you are prospecting you have to look at everything and make your decisions on the information you have available to you.

Facebook

Don't forget to take a closer look at the more social of the social networks, a lot of these ask for company information when you do your profile, with this information you can search for companies and get lists of people who work for them which could give you the in that you need when making contact, remember that people in the company can sometimes provide useful information on the people you should really be talking to, don't be afraid to ask for the information you need to have.

Many companies are now including Facebook pages for themselves and you could gain some insight or even possibly start a conversation thread on the page and get to know others that work at the organization. Remember you need to improvise and think out of the box to move your closer to your goal.

The Gatekeeper / Receptionist

One thing that you are going to come up with very early in your Cold Calling is a run in with the Gatekeeper, that is what we call the person whose job it is to screen incoming calls so as to not let sales calls or other unwanted calls to get through to the people who are working and making the company money. There are a few ways to get through the gatekeeper and they are:

You can turn the Gatekeeper into your Ally, by being honest about what you are calling about and who you are and what your company represents and they may see the benefit to your call and help to point you in the right direction. Of course that doesn't always work out well either, most times they will shut you down anyway but it is worth a shot. If you have some charisma you may want to try and establish a rapport with the gatekeeper, again its worth a shot but could backfire if you are not careful.

You may want to try calling just before normal business hours or right after normal business hours end, this way you may end up speaking with someone from security or may have to deal with an automated phone system which may give you the opportunity to get to the person you are trying to call as some people come in early or stay late and during those times they may very well be sitting at their desk trying to catch up on work that has built up while they were doing other things during normal business hours, keep in mind that they are probably busy so be brief and get to the point of your call, or if they are busy maybe ask them what is a good time to call back and get there extension or direct line to avoid the gatekeeper entirely.

Some gatekeepers are good at their job and others are not so one way to change the subject is to try and get them to give you additional information about the company or who might be the right person to speak to about this. Often times they will transfer you to someone else who may be more friendly to your position, but often they just give you over to their own salespeople who have no interest in what you are selling most of the time, either that or they give you to Human Resources which usually gets you nowhere fast.

If I am calling blind I will usually ask to speak to someone in a specific department rather than a person, this sometimes catches them off guard and will put you through, it is worth a try if you find yourself up against a gatekeeper.

One thing that is important is that no matter what you need to be nice and of course you need to be polite, you get a lot more with sugar then vinegar as grandma always used to tell me growing up. That is still true today so don't be a jerk, they are just doing their job just like you are trying to do yours.

You could also state right up front that you are not sure who you should talk to and let them decide, worse case that gets you to someone else who may be more helpful.

Either way the gatekeeper can be a formidable obstacle to overcome and with practice you will find things that work and things that don't, make sure you add the things that work to your toolbox.

Always treat the receptionist as a very important individual. Get to know what is important to them. Give them company "Toys". If there on secretaries day, bring a flower, or candy . Treat them special.

You're Companies Website

If you have any control over your company's website, even if you have just the ability to make suggestions, it would be important for your company's website had the ability to capture information. You can do this through survey's for a discount, or even a mailing list which can be quite simple and at least you would capture their email address which is better than most. Anytime you can get a customer to come to you makes your job that much easier to do.

Conclusion

If you implement the ideas contained in this book with conviction and manage your time appropriately you should be able to see tangible results on your efforts. Nothing is accomplished overnight and I am certainly not stating that you will be a better salesperson because of the information we have given you. What you will be is better informed and will have a change in mindset that will allow you to utilize commonsense techniques to build a better mouse trap.

All industries are different and quite the same as well, the fact of the matter is that it is still up to you to make a change and place your foot on the path to a better tomorrow. Either way it is going to take hard work, you will have to get your hands dirty but it will pay off in the end. The simple truth is it is a numbers game the more contacts you have the better chance percentage and statistic wise you will turn potential customers into real customers. You will continue to improve your abilities in communication and research. You will probably find a half a dozen new and different ways to locate new contacts that I myself haven't even thought of, but either way you will be working towards the goal of what you want and need and that is more sales and more customers to sell to.

Good Luck and Keep on Prospecting……

If you have any questions or would just like to get in touch with me drop me a line.

Jesse Rogers

Jesserogers01@gmail.com

About the Author:

Jesse Rogers was born and raised in Queens New York and lived there until he came of age. He achieved a 4.0 GPA and graduated with Honors and on the Dean's List with a degree in Electronics / Computer Science. Working in the Electronics Field for a Military Simulator Company in Florida, he was financially forced to obtain a second job to take care of his family. Working a second job in telemarketing he came to the understanding of how powerful it was for someone to be able to communicate clearly and with confidence utilizing the telephone. This understanding soon overlapped into his careered position and he realized that the pathway to success in business lead away from hands on work in his chosen field and onto a pathway that lead at first to a B2B Inside Sales position in Technical Sales to an Outside Sales Position serving the Electronic Manufacturing Industry. With his knowledge in Electronics and his understanding of quality customer service he embarked on this new path with diligence accomplishing a successful career in Business to Business Sales.

www.ingramcontent.com/pod-product-compliance
Lightning Source LLC
Chambersburg PA
CBHW051336170526
45166CB00002B/839